Saving M...
Birds

Ben Nussbaum

Smithsonian

Contributing Author

Allison Duarte

Consultants

Brian S. Evans, Ph.D.
Ecologist
Smithsonian Conservation Biology Institute's Migratory Bird Center

Mary Deinlein, M.S.
Bird Conservation Education Specialist
Smithsonian Conservation Biology Institute's Migratory Bird Center

Sara Hallager
Curator of Birds
Department of Animal Care Sciences
National Zoological Park

Stephanie Anastasopoulos, M.Ed.
TOSA, STREAM Integration
Solana Beach School District

Publishing Credits

Rachelle Cracchiolo, M.S.Ed., *Publisher*
Conni Medina, M.A.Ed., *Managing Editor*
Diana Kenney, M.A.Ed., NBCT, *Content Director*
Véronique Bos, *Creative Director*
Robin Erickson, *Art Director*
Michelle Jovin, M.A., *Associate Editor*
Mindy Duits, *Senior Graphic Designer*
Smithsonian Science Education Center

Image Credits: p.7 (top) SPL/Science Source; p.9 (top) North Wind Picture Archives/Alamy; p.11 (top), p.13 (bottom), p.14 (all), p.15, p.16 (inserts), p.20 (bottom), p.21 (middle), p.24 (right) © Smithsonian; p.25 (top) Jason Smalley Photography/Alamy; all other images from iStock and/or Shutterstock.

Library of Congress Cataloging-in-Publication Data

Names: Nussbaum, Ben, 1975- author.
Title: Saving migratory birds / Ben Nussbaum.
Description: Huntington Beach, CA : Teacher Created Materials, Inc., [2019] |
   Audience: Grade 4 to 6. | Includes index. |
Identifiers: LCCN 2018018104 (print) | LCCN 2018019641 (ebook) | ISBN
   9781493869480 (E-book) | ISBN 9781493867080 (paperback)
Subjects: LCSH: Migratory birds--Conservation--Juvenile literature.
Classification: LCC QL698.9 (ebook) | LCC QL698.9 .N87 2019 (print) | DDC
   598.156/8--dc23
LC record available at https://lccn.loc.gov/2018018104

☀ Smithsonian

Teacher Created Materials

5301 Oceanus Drive
Huntington Beach, CA 92649-1030
www.tcmpub.com
ISBN 978-1-4938-6708-0

Table of Contents

Heron Here, Heron There

Every spring, a flock of black-crowned night herons arrives at Smithsonian's National Zoo in Washington, DC. The herons build nests high in trees, choose **mates**, and raise their young. Zoo staff feed the birds mice and fish. The herons are noisy. Sometimes, they are even smelly—young herons vomit to **deter** predators when they feel threatened.

Black-crowned night herons have been returning to this spot for at least a hundred years. Bit by bit, the Zoo has grown up around the birds. In August or September, the herons fly away. Almost overnight, the loud flock is replaced by silence.

Where the herons go has always been a mystery. But now, new technology lets scientists track the birds. During the summer, trackers are strapped to a few herons. As the herons travel, the devices tell scientists where the birds are located. Scientists know not only where the herons spend winter but also how they get there.

All over the world, people who study birds are using new technology to answer old questions. And it's happening just in time—many **migratory** birds need humans to give them a helping hand.

Almost half of all bird **species** migrate.

A black-crowned
night heron
catches a fish.

Night herons get their name
because they are active at night.

black-crowned
night heron

Migration Sensation

Many animals move to different locations when the weather changes. Birds are the champions of the animal world when it comes to finding the best spots to live throughout the year.

The small Arctic tern travels from the Arctic at the top of the globe to the Antarctic at the bottom, giving it the longest migration of any animal! The bar-tailed godwit is another record holder. It soars over the Pacific Ocean for eight days and nights without stopping during its migration from New Zealand to Alaska.

Some birds have much shorter migrations. For example, some spend the summer high on a mountain where the weather is cool, but they spend the rest of the year at a lower elevation.

Migration has many benefits. Think about a lake in northern Europe. During the summer, it is full of fish. Thick clouds of insects hover in the air. Flowers bloom and trees are green. For water birds, such as loons and ducks, the lake is a great place to have a family. Food is plentiful, which allows these birds to build nests, lay eggs, and protect their young.

In the winter, that same lake is frozen solid. All the water birds are far away, in warmer places.

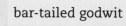

bar-tailed godwit

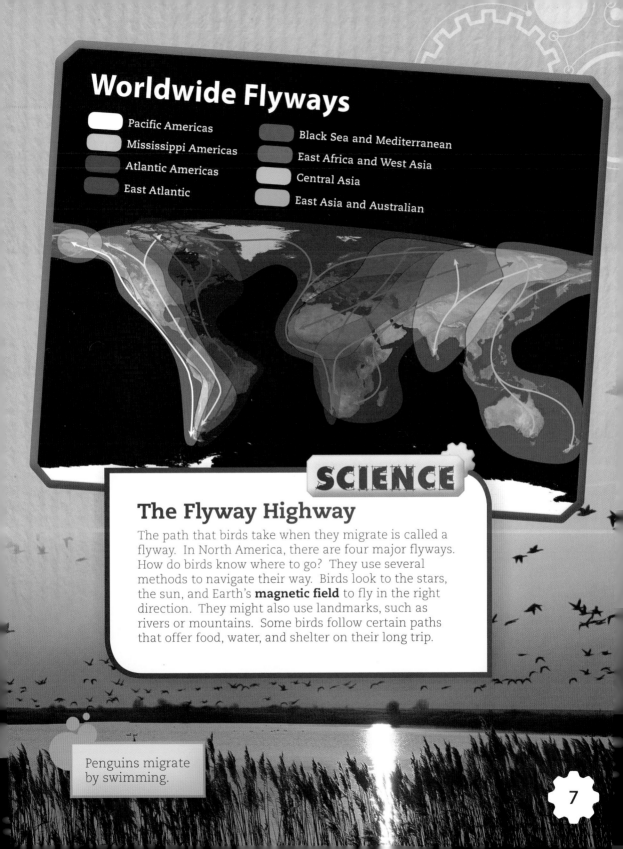

Worldwide Flyways

- Pacific Americas
- Mississippi Americas
- Atlantic Americas
- East Atlantic
- Black Sea and Mediterranean
- East Africa and West Asia
- Central Asia
- East Asia and Australian

SCIENCE

The Flyway Highway

The path that birds take when they migrate is called a flyway. In North America, there are four major flyways. How do birds know where to go? They use several methods to navigate their way. Birds look to the stars, the sun, and Earth's **magnetic field** to fly in the right direction. They might also use landmarks, such as rivers or mountains. Some birds follow certain paths that offer food, water, and shelter on their long trip.

Penguins migrate by swimming.

Migration is not easy. Bad weather can push birds off course. They have to survive predators and hunters. The journey is so hard on their bodies that some birds starve.

Birds are also harmed by pollution, including toxic chemicals. They can be trapped in fishing nets or crash into buildings. Loss of habitat is a huge problem as well.

Although most species of migratory birds aren't close to extinction, many are under stress. When a species that migrates is in trouble, conservationists face a big challenge. Protecting an animal that lives in one place is hard enough. Protecting an animal that lives in two places is more difficult.

Bald Eagle Distribution

- resident
- summer migration
- winter migration
- visit on migration only

The bald eagle is the **emblem** of the United States, but many of them spend their summers in Canada before migrating south.

This 1870s wood carving shows hunters shooting passenger pigeons.

The passenger pigeon is one extinct migratory species. Once, these pigeons were the most common bird in North America. They lived together in huge flocks that were so big they took hours to pass overhead. In summer, the birds could be spotted as far north as Canada. In winter, they lived as far south as Florida.

Farmers killed many passenger pigeons to protect their crops. Hunters killed many of the birds, too. Forests the birds needed were cut down to make farms. When living together in a big community was no longer possible, they stopped nesting and raising young. In 1914, the last passenger pigeon died.

A Rare Warbler

Kirtland's warblers are small birds, but people are making a big effort to help them. Warblers spend the winter in the Bahamas. They spend the summer in and around Michigan in an unusual **ecosystem** called a pine barren. This is the only place that warblers build nests.

Kirtland's warblers require a certain tree, called jack pine. These trees are common in pine barrens. Pine barrens occur where soil is dry and **acidic**, often near water. Pine barrens need forest fires. Some species of pine trees have waxy pinecones that need fires to spread their seeds. Fires add these new **nutrients** to the soil and expose existing nutrients. They also burn tall trees, such as oaks, opening up space for new pine trees to grow.

When people started fighting forest fires, pine barrens became less common. Without this rare habitat, Kirtland's warblers struggled to survive. At times, there were fewer than 500 of these birds in the world, making them an **endangered** species.

Luckily, people realized what was happening. Now, conservationists manage pine barrens by cutting down old trees to make room for new, healthy trees. But Kirtland's warblers like pine trees that are between about 5 and 20 years old. So, conservationists have to be careful to leave some older trees.

Nashville warbler

Nashville warblers, brown thrashers, and clay-colored sparrows also thrive in the Kirtland's warblers' protected habitat.

Kirtland's warbler

About 50 species of warblers live in the United States. Many are brightly colored.

black-throated blue warbler

Blackburnian warbler

jack pine

12

A Unique Habitat

Today, areas in pine barren habitats have been set aside for Kirtland's warblers. These birds are now a success story. There are now about 4,500 Kirtland's warblers around the world. Scientists from Smithsonian have been studying these birds. They've seen firsthand why they need pine barrens.

Having babies is a lot of work for a warbler. Building a nest takes five to six days. Then, the mother bird spends about two weeks sitting on her eggs. Once the babies hatch, they stay in the nest for another 10 days. The parents still have another month of work left, watching over and protecting their young as they explore the world.

All that work means that warblers need a resource-rich environment to raise their young. The pine barrens habitat swarms with insects in the spring. Best of all, blueberries thrive in the acidic soil of the pine barrens. Kirtland's warblers love to devour these berries.

Pine barrens are the perfect environment for other reasons. In this habitat, pine trees grow closely together. Kirtland's warblers build their nests on the ground. The short, crowded pines protect the nests. Young warblers hide by matching the colors of their unique environment. Plenty of low branches are vital for the young birds that hop around on the ground before eventually making it to the branches of the pine trees.

one-day-old
Kirtland's warbler

Kirtland's warbler with a radio transmitter

Adult Kirtland's warblers furiously protect their fledglings. They sometimes even pretend to be injured to draw attention away from their young.

seven-day-old nestling with a radio transmitter

Leaving the Nest

One summer, scientists attached radio transmitters to some of the young warblers to learn more about the **fledgling** stage. This is the period when birds have left the nest but are still helped by their parents.

The devices were attached when the birds were seven days old. Each bird's transmitter **broadcast** on a different **frequency**. This way, scientists could tell where each bird was based on its radio signal.

About five days after the transmitters were attached, the young birds left their nests. About 35 days later, the batteries died. This is about when the fledglings became fully independent of their parents. Later, the transmitters fell off the birds.

Scientists learned that fledglings do not go very far from where they hatch. They also learned that the first few days out of the nest are the most dangerous for the young birds.

Scientists found several birds buried in the dirt. This is a sign that cats might have killed them. These pets can easily catch the birds before they are able to fly.

This information is extremely valuable. It will help in making a plan to keep the warbler population in the pine barrens healthy.

tools for tracking birds

Scientists from Smithsonian have also tracked the warblers as they migrate. One way they've done so is by using geolocators. These devices measure light. With this information, scientists can figure out the exact times the sun set and rose each day that a bird wore the device. Then, they can figure out the bird's location in the world.

Geolocators weigh less than a paper clip. Even a small bird like a warbler can easily carry one. Scientists tag a bird in the summer, and then find the same bird again the next summer. They take off the tracker and download its information.

A scientist removes a geolocator from a Kirtland's warbler.

a Kirtland's warbler with a geolocator on its back

MATHEMATICS

Carry That Weight

Birds are lightweight animals, so it is important for trackers to be light too. One rule of thumb that scientists use is that a tracker should never weigh more than 5 percent of a bird's body weight. A Kirtland's warbler weighs about 13 grams (0.5 ounces), a little less than three nickels. Based on the rule, a tracker for a Kirtland's warbler should weigh no more than 0.65 g (0.02 oz.). That's about half the weight of a paper clip.

In some cases, scientists can't find birds they had tagged earlier. Sometimes, the devices break. Even with these limitations, most locators offer a lot of information. Using them, scientists were able to track the warblers on their journeys for the first time.

Scientists recently started using a new way to track the birds. They attach radio tags to the birds. The tags send out pings on a radio frequency. When the birds pass by certain radio towers, the towers pick up the signal. That tells scientists that the birds are near the towers. It does not give scientists an exact location, but it gives them a general idea of the path the birds are taking.

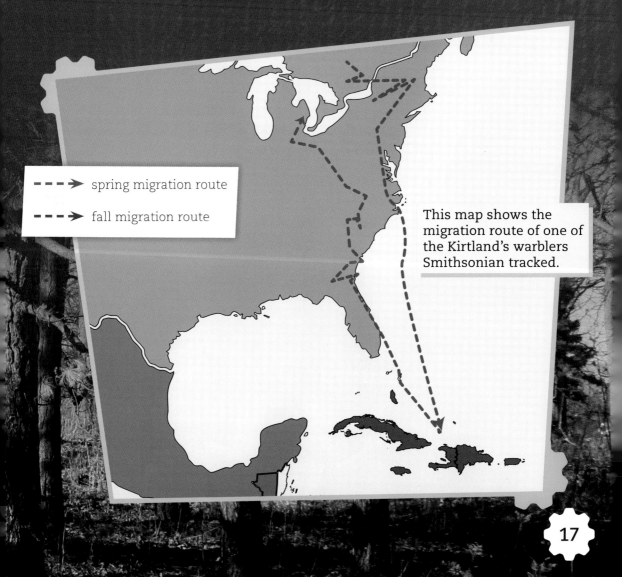

- - - ➤ spring migration route

- - - ➤ fall migration route

This map shows the migration route of one of the Kirtland's warblers Smithsonian tracked.

Pelican Power

The brown pelican is a large bird that lives in coastal areas. It dives into the ocean and scoops up fish with the massive pouch in its bill. In 1970, it was listed as an endangered species. One problem the birds faced was **pesticides**. Farmers use these products to keep insects from eating their crops.

Some pesticides can be very toxic to other animals. They get washed off plants and go into the soil. Eventually, they make their way into rivers, lakes, and oceans. Fish become loaded with poisonous chemicals. For birds that eat fish, this is very bad news. The brown pelican almost went extinct, but it has **rebounded**.

Most brown pelicans live on the coasts of the Atlantic and Pacific Oceans. The weather stays warm enough that many of the birds do not need to migrate. Of the brown pelicans that *do* migrate, not much is known about the route they take or how long their migration lasts.

Gathering information about pelicans is still important. That way, people will be prepared if pelicans face a crisis in the future.

brown pelican chicks in a nest

A brown pelican catches a fish.

Brown Pelican Distribution

resident

on migration

Brown pelicans can live long lives. The oldest ever found was 43 years old!

Some brown pelicans nest in the **marshy** islands in Maryland's Chesapeake Bay. Scientists from Smithsonian put trackers on five of these pelicans. They used devices that weighed 65 g (2.3 oz.)—about as much as a small apple. These trackers are solar powered. They can survive extreme heat and cold. They also offer incredible information. They communicate with the worldwide GPS system. By doing so, they can pinpoint where the birds are within 15 meters (50 feet). One bird wore a unique tracker. It kept a record of the bird's dives into the ocean.

As the GPS data arrived, scientists input it into a website. Anyone could track the pelicans at the Migratory Connectivity Project site. It showed each bird as a dot on a map. It included a history of where the birds had been.

In the first year of the study, the pelicans spent a lot of time in the bay. They visited many islands and areas on the coast. In winter, the birds did not migrate very far. Three of the five birds flew to North Carolina before the trackers stopped working.

Scientists at Smithsonian continue to study this species. Often, years of science are needed before a migration pattern is understood.

Smithsonian scientists attach a tracker to a brown pelican.

GPS satellite

Smithsonian researcher Autumn-Lynn Harrison holds a brown pelican.

Doppler radar station

TECHNOLOGY

A Different Forecast

Weather forecasters use Doppler radar. It works by sending out radio waves that bounce off objects in the waves' paths. Some of the waves echo back to the radar stations. The information gathered shows any rain or snow in the air. The radio waves sometimes bounce off birds. Normally, this information is ignored. Now, conservationists use it. By filtering out information about rain and snow, they can get a picture of when migrations start.

Helping Hands

People are helping migratory birds in many ways. One development is the rise of the citizen scientist. People who care about birds can be part of the scientific community. It doesn't take any special training.

One way people can help is through a website called eBird. People can report when and where they went bird watching and the species they saw. Because many people take part, the data has a lot of value to scientists. They can analyze it to find which species need help. The data collected by eBird is also very useful in figuring out what paths birds take when migrating.

The Smithsonian Institution has a citizen scientist program too. It is called Neighborhood Nestwatch. People in a number of cities record which birds they see in their own backyards. They watch bird nests to determine how long birds survive in different environments.

Many organizations also track monarch butterflies, another long-distance migrator.

A mother blackbird feeds her chicks.

black-naped monarch

The Motus Wildlife Tracking System takes the idea of being a citizen scientist to the next level. Motus tracks birds and other animals through radio towers. Many towers are on private land. People volunteer to put them up and take care of them.

Students can help too. Journey North tracks birds as they move in the spring and fall. Many families and schools take part in Journey North by reporting their sightings.

Another way people can help is with the choices they make when shopping. For example, most coffee farms aren't very good for birds. Forests are cut down to make room for coffee plants. The Smithsonian Bird Friendly® program is working to reward coffee farmers who grow their beans in the shade of tall trees that offer shelter and food for birds. Some brands of coffee carry the Smithsonian "Bird Friendly" label. People can trust that those coffee farms try to help birds.

Another easy fix is to prevent birds from crashing into windows. Lights can attract birds. Tired migrating birds sometimes collide with tall, lit-up apartment buildings. For people who live in tall buildings, a simple solution is to turn off lights at night. Many types of tapes and stickers can also be placed on large windows to keep birds safe. They are available online or at stores that specialize in bird supplies.

Anyone with a yard can help migrating birds too. Birds need water. A birdbath can be an **oasis**. Even a hollowed-out boulder that catches some rainwater can make a big difference. Plants that are native to an area are great for wildlife. Variety is important too. Tall trees, small trees, shrubs, and even small amounts of decaying leaves or wood all work to create nice homes for animals, especially birds.

coffee plants

Robert Rice (far left) is the director of the Smithsonian Bird Friendly program.

Garden Party

Designing a garden to attract birds takes some thought and planning. Start with plants native to an area. Have a variety of plants that provide seeds, fruit, or flowers and that come in different colors. There should be layers of plants since some birds feed and nest closer to the ground while others like plants and trees that are higher. Build or buy bird feeders and make sure there is food year-round. Your garden will surely attract some feathered friends!

Migratory Marvels

The migration mystery of the black-crowned night herons has finally been solved. After staff strapped transmitters to a few of the birds at Smithsonian's National Zoo, they waited to see where the birds would go.

Soon, one of the birds took off. It headed to South Carolina, then Florida. About two weeks after the bird left the Zoo, it left Florida and then, after a few hours, landed in Cuba. People at the Zoo always wondered how far south their herons went. They had an answer.

The transmitters continued to work in the spring. When the herons started moving north, the Zoo knew that the migration had started. The loud flock's arrival was welcome and exciting as always. The fact that zoo staff tracked a few birds as they arrived made it even more special.

The herons are just one of at least four thousand species of birds that migrate. They range from giant cranes to tiny finches. Some of the rarest birds migrate, and so do some of the most common. Assisting these travelers is important.

Luckily, black-crowned night herons are not in trouble. Scientists are ready to help if that ever changes. Armed with information, they can figure out the best way to lend a hand.

ENGINEERING

Artificial Islands

One way to help birds is to put artificial floating islands in ponds or lakes. One company makes islands from recycled plastics that can be covered with plants. The plants' roots dangle into the water through holes in the island. Either a rope or a chain and anchor keep the islands in place. The islands are **buoyant** enough to support a lot of weight. Some islands are even large enough to hold a picnic table and several people.

migration of three tagged
black-crowned night herons

Smith

Jackson

Parker

27

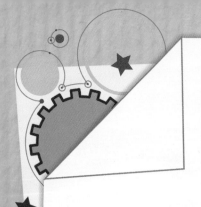

STEAM CHALLENGE

Define the Problem

Migration is a risky mission! Migratory birds face many challenges. Stress, lack of food and water, extreme weather, and predators are all dangers. Scientists and engineers have found new ways to monitor and help these birds. Your task is to design and build a model of an artificial island that can provide a safe space for birds during their seasonal journey.

Constraints: You may only use four types of materials to build your model.

Criteria: Your model island must float in water while supporting five washers.

Research and Brainstorm

What types of environmental factors cause birds to migrate? How can people help migrating birds? What types of plants and flowers do migrating birds like?

Design and Build

Sketch your artificial island design. What purpose will each part serve? What materials will work best? Build the model.

Test and Improve

Test your model by placing it in water. Add the washers to the surface of the model. Did it work? How can you improve it? Modify your design and try again.

Reflect and Share

What types of materials can you use to create a stronger model? What other ways can you test your model? Can you think of any other purposes for artificial islands?

Glossary

acidic—a type of soil that contains potentially harmful chemicals and can affect plant life

broadcast—sent information

buoyant—able to float in water or air

conservationists—people who want to protect nature and animals

deter—to discourage

ecosystem—a community of living and nonliving things in a particular environment

emblem—a symbol

endangered—very rare and in danger of dying out completely

extinction—the state of no longer existing

fledgling—a bird that has left the nest but is not fully independent

frequency—a certain wavelength on which sounds can be transmitted

habitat—the area where a plant or an animal lives

magnetic field—an invisible region around a magnetic object which influences other magnetic objects around it

marshy—wet, swampy

mates—pairs of animals that breed together

migratory—passing from one place to another in a repeating pattern

nutrients—substances that help people, animals, or plants grow

oasis—something that provides relief or a pleasant change

pesticides—chemicals used to kill insects and plants

rebounded—recovered

species—a group of animals that are similar and can produce young together

toxic—poisonous

Index

CAREER ADVICE
from Smithsonian

Do you want to help migratory birds?
Here are some tips to get you started.

"The two things I love most are birds and talking about birds. I plan a festival about migratory birds and create fun activities. I get to wear a lot of hats every day: teacher, creator, inventor, and birder." —*Mary Deinlein, Smithsonian Migratory Bird Center Education Specialist*

"I first knew I wanted to study birds and wildlife when I was six years old. This was after I experienced an up-close-and-personal look at a black-capped chickadee. Today, I travel through Central and South America and the Caribbean to study birds and their habitats." —*Pete Marra, Conservation Scientist and Director of the Smithsonian Migratory Bird Center*